GREAT TALES FROM LONG AGO

THE TRAVELS OF MARCO POLO

Retold by Felicity Trotman
Illustrated by Daniel Woods

Methuen Children's Books
in association with Belitha Press Ltd.

Note: Rustichello's manuscript of Marco Polo's adventures was so popular that it soon fell to pieces – but it had been copied by several different hands. In the copying mistakes and additional material crept in: modern editors of *The Travels of Marco Polo* try to piece together the original story from at least half-a-dozen different versions. Marco Polo was born in 1254, and left for China in 1271. He returned to Venice in 1295, and died, aged seventy, in 1324. For the last part of his life he had been a peaceful merchant, but as he lay dying he murmured "I never told the half of what I saw . . ."

F.T.

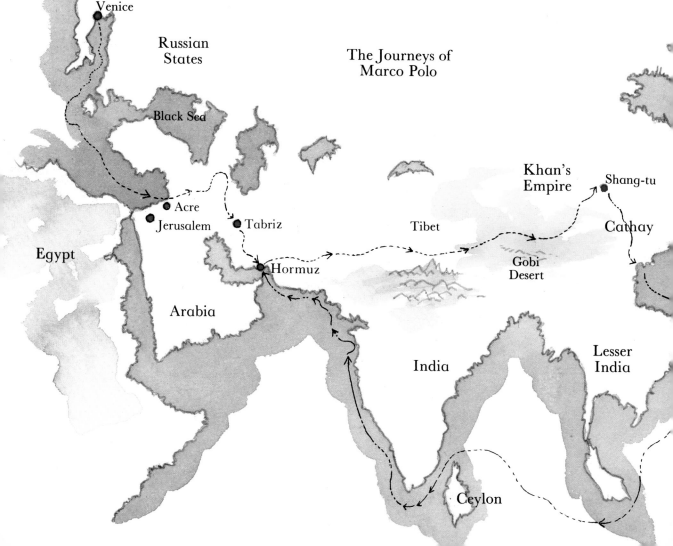

The Journeys of Marco Polo

Venice · Russian States · Black Sea · Acre · Jerusalem · Egypt · Tabriz · Arabia · Hormuz · Tibet · India · Gobi Desert · Khan's Empire · Shang-tu · Cathay · Lesser India · Ceylon

SEVEN HUNDRED YEARS AGO, VENICE AND GENOA WERE AT WAR.
Two men met in prison in Genoa.
One was the commander of a Venetian galley,
the other was a writer from Pisa.
They spent their time talking,
and the Venetian told the Pisan some very strange stories.
"Messer Marco," said the writer,
"to pass the time in prison,
why do we not make a book of your adventures?
Tell me your story from the beginning,
and I will write it down."
"An excellent idea, Rustichello," said Marco.

I**T ALL STARTED WHEN I WAS A BOY.**
I grew up in Venice, in a family of merchants.
My father and uncle had gone away on a journey
and for years we had no news of them but suddenly,
when I was fifteen, they came home.
They said they had been across the world,
to a country called Cathay.
It was ruled by a great and powerful monarch, Khan Kubilai,
who sent them home with a letter to the Pope,
asking for a hundred wise men
who could teach his people, the Tartars, about Christianity.
He also wanted some holy oil from the lamp
in the church of the Holy Sepulchre in Jerusalem.

SADLY, WHEN MY FATHER AND UNCLE REACHED VENICE,
there was no Pope. The old one had died,
and a new one had not yet been chosen.
They waited and waited – but at last decided
that they could wait no longer.
The Khan would be angry if they took too long on his errand.
To my great delight, they said I could go with them.
Imagine! I was seventeen when we started,
and was going on an adventure
greater than anyone in Europe could dream of.

WE SAILED TO ACRE, IN THE HOLY LAND,
where we found a friend, the Papal Legate Theobald.
He was most interested in our mission,
and arranged for us to get the holy oil from Jerusalem.
As we journeyed north from Acre to Ayas, the news came
that there was a new Pope –
none other than our friend Theobald,
who was now Pope Gregory X.
We went back to Acre immediately.
Even the Pope could not find a hundred wise men,
but he ordered two learned friars to go with us.
He also sent a message for the Khan, and costly gifts.

OUR FIRST SETBACK CAME WHEN WE FOUND WAR PREVENTED US
from travelling the way we wanted to go.
Our two friars were not used to this.
They were so frightened they turned back home.
This was a sad loss, but we decided to go on.
We detoured to avoid the war, travelling through Armenia, Georgia
and south along the western shores of the Caspian Sea into Persia.
At Baku, near the Georgian border, there is a spring which gushes oil.
It cannot be eaten, but it can be burned,
and used as a salve for men and animals with skin diseases.
Men come many miles to collect this oil.

M Y FATHER AND UNCLE HAD DISCOVERED THAT
in Southern Persia there was a town called Hormuz,
from which ships could be taken to India
and then on to Cathay.
We therefore travelled south, though the road was difficult.
There were regions where no grass grew to feed our horses,
and the wells and springs were a long way apart.
There were also many bandits and, to try and protect travellers,
it was customary to collect them up into groups
and escort them across dangerous country with an armed guard.

At one place, not far from Hormuz,
we were attacked by the bandits called Karaunas –
they are famous for their ferocity, and also for their magic!
They can raise a fog, and attack
when their victims are frightened and confused in the darkness.
But we were lucky, and escaped when they attacked.

WHEN WE REACHED HORMUZ IT WAS SCORCHINGLY HOT.
All the fruits and vegetables are ripened and finished by
March, except the dates, which last until May.
Then even they are shrivelled up!
We tried to find a ship to take us to India,
but when we examined them we were horrified!
They were small, with no decks
and were sewn together with coconut-husk thread,
for the shipwrights had no iron nails.
Since they had no pitch to caulk the seams,
they were smeared over with reeking fish-oil.
We discovered that many of them sank in the stormy Indian Ocean!
So we had to decide to carry on by land.

OUR WAY LAY ACROSS A VERY NASTY DESERT,
which took us seven days to cross.
The little water we found made us all very ill,
so we were glad to get to a town
with a spring of fresh water, where we rested.
Now we headed east and north, climbing upwards all the time.
We reached the province of Badakhshan, where we stayed some time.
I had been ill, but the good air made me completely well.

WHEN WE LEFT THIS PLACE, WE CLIMBED FOR EIGHTEEN DAYS.
Then we reached the plain of Pamir,
which took us twelve days to cross.
No one lives here, and there is no shelter,
so the traveller must take everything he needs with him.
It is so high and so cold that no birds fly in the sky.
I noticed that our fires did not burn so brightly.
The flames were a different colour.
Our food did not cook well.

FROM THE PLAIN OF PAMIR, THE ROAD SLOPES DOWNWARDS.
At last we came to a big city called Lop,
an important place for all travellers going east to stop,
for then comes a great desert.
At its narrowest point from west to east, it takes a month to cross it
and there is nothing to eat,
only a little water every now and then.

Travellers must stay together when crossing this desert.
There are strange noises here
and if a man loiters, or falls asleep, and drops behind his party,
he will think he hears their voices,
and in following the sounds, will be utterly lost.
Some people have seen what appears to be
a great host of men coming toward them.
Thinking they are robbers, they leave the path to try and escape –
but again, become hopelessly lost.
So careful travellers keep close together,
and when they go to sleep at night they put up a little sign
pointing in the direction they want to travel on the morrow.
They tie small bells round the necks of their pack animals,
to keep them from straying.
When we completed our crossing of the Gobi Desert,
we were at last in the huge lands ruled directly by the Great Khan.
Our travels had already lasted three and a half years.

THE KHAN RECEIVED US WITH PLEASURE
and entertained us well at his summer palace at Shang-tu.
He questioned us about our journeying,
and received his presents with delight.
Then he noticed me. "Who is that?" he asked.
"Sire," said my father, "he is my son and your servant."
We were well looked after at the palace – actually a huge tent,
made of split bamboo canes with silk guy-ropes,
pitched in the middle of a beautiful stretch of parkland.
He also had another palace in Peking,
a vast, magnificent building covered in gold and silver
and with a hall big enough to serve a meal to six thousand men.
Kubilai was very interested in magic,
and some of the things the magicians did were most impressive.
We saw his filled cup fly from the table into his hand!

WE SAW MANY WONDERFUL THINGS WHILE WE LIVED IN CATHAY. There was a kind of mineral, called salamander, which was dug out of a hillside. It was fibrous, and when beaten together formed a sort of cloth, which resisted fire completely. When at last we went home, we took some of this and presented it to the Pope.

ONE THING THAT SURPRISED ME VERY MUCH was that people do not use gold and silver for money – but paper! It is all very carefully organised, with different sizes of paper for different values. Seven officials stamp each piece with their personal seals, and then the Khan's representative stamps on the top the Khan's seal, in vermilion. Then the money is valid – and anyone who tries to forge it is executed. Everywhere we went in Kubilai's domains, we found people using this paper money. The Khan kept all the gold and silver for himself.

THE KHAN ALSO HAS A VERY CLEVER SYSTEM OF POSTS.
From Peking, roads run to many provinces.
At intervals of twenty-five miles along these roads are posting
stations, where messengers can find lodgings and fresh horses.
For urgent despatches, special riders are used:
they sound a horn as they approach each post station,
and fresh horses are waiting for them when they arrive.
By changing horses quickly, and riding on,
they can cover up to three hundred miles a day!
And even in the remotest parts of the country,
the Khan has established more than 10,000 of these stations,
with stabling for more than 200,000 horses.
Thus messages can be sent safely and quickly
throughout the whole of the Khan's realms.

KUBILAI APPOINTED ME AS
an assistant commissioner to his Privy Council,
for I could speak (and write) four of the Tartar languages.
When the Khan sent me out on missions,
I made a point of noting interesting things
about the lands and peoples I came across
so that I could report back
on more than just the business I had been sent on.
One one occasion the Khan said,
"If this young man lives to reach full manhood,
he will certainly prove himself a man of sound judgement and worth."
I was very proud of this tribute.

IN THE KHAN'S SERVICE I MADE MANY JOURNEYS THROUGH CHINA.
I also went abroad, notably to Bengal and Burma,
a journey of six months.
I went through Tibet, which had been devastated by war,
and was most impressed at my journey's end to see elephants fighting!
Our Tartar archers could overcome elephants,
though their horses were frightened, and could not be used.

IN BURMA I SAW BEAUTIFUL TOWERS MADE OF GOLD AND SILVER,
and covered in bells, which tinkled whenever the wind blew.
The Tartars always respected other people's religions,
and had left these towers untouched.
My other great journey was to Ceylon and India.
Khan Kubilai was most interested in religion,
and had heard that in Ceylon were a tooth and a begging bowl
that had belonged to Buddha.
I was sent to get them.

WE SAILED FROM AMOY, ON FOUR-MASTED OCEAN-GOING SHIPS.
We sailed along the coast,
crossing the China Sea in two months,
and stopping at many islands, including Sumatra,
where we were delayed for five months because of the monsoon season.
Here I found a tree which dripped wine,
and another tree whose trunk was full of flour,
which is very good to eat.
Ceylon is exquisite –
the finest island for its size in the world.
I obtained the tooth and the begging bowl
but the king would not sell me a superb giant ruby
for any treasure that I could offer him.
From Ceylon I crossed into India,
and explored some of the southern regions.
Maarbar is a centre for pearl-fishing:
divers bring up big sea-oysters from the sea bed.
Quantities are gathered like this, and they are large and lustrous.
Motupalli is ruled by a wise queen, a widow much loved by her people.
This is where diamonds come from,
though the area where the diamonds are is very dangerous,
being infested with poisonous snakes.
I was told that lumps of meat are thrown
into the valley where the diamonds are.
The stones stick to the meat,
which is seized and carried off by white eagles.
Thus men can get at the diamonds
without having to go near the snakes.

FOR SOME TIME MY FATHER AND UNCLE AND I
had talked about going home.
The Khan was growing old,
and we knew that his successor might not be so friendly to foreigners.
Also, we wanted to see our home and family again!
We had asked the Khan for permission to leave,
but he had always refused.
Then came our opportunity.
Kubilai's great-nephew, Arghun, ruled in Persia.
His queen had died, but her last wish was
that her husband's new wife should be from her own family.
Consequently, he sent an embassy to Kubilai.
A princess was chosen – seventeen-year-old Kokachin.
The party set off by land,
but could not return because the road was blocked by a war.

T HEY ARRIVED BACK IN PEKING
just as I got back from my Indian trip.
Of course, the Persians were extremely interested
in my account of the sea-route there –
and in the end, Khan Kubilai agreed to let us go,
to take the Persians and the princess home.
He gave us two of his gold passports,
and many messages to rulers of the west.
He gave us a fleet of fourteen ships, and food for two years.
Again, it was a long journey, and full of danger.
There were storms and pirates and illnesses,
and of the six hundred men who started out,
only eighteen reached Hormuz.

BUT AT LAST WE FELT WE WERE REALLY NEARING HOME.
This time we headed for the Black Sea, and at Trebizond
embarked on a voyage that eventually ended in Venice.
And can you imagine? No one recognised us!
Our journey had taken us away for twenty-three years,
and our Tartar clothes not only looked strange,
but were all worn and stained from travelling.
Our family would have turned us from the door as beggars –
but we invited them all to a lavish banquet.
During this, we tore open the seams of our garments.
This is where we had stored our riches,
and the family were amazed as streams of jewels poured onto the floor!
After that you may be sure we were welcomed back with much joy!

RUSTICHELLO FINISHED WRITING FROM MARCO POLO'S DICTATION. "This is an extraordinary story," he said. "Most people will not believe it."
"I know," said Marco. "People nickname me 'Marco Millions' because they say I exaggerate so much.
But I swear to you that it is all true.
There has never been a man yet
who has explored so much of the world as I,
Marco Polo, a citizen of Venice."